BASIC ESSENT

BASIC ✳ ESSENTIALS (R)

FLY FISHING

MICHAEL RUTTER

The
Globe
Pequot
press

Guilford, Connecticut

Cover photo by David White/Index Stock Imagery
Cover design by Lana Mullen
Text and layout design by Casey Shain
Illustrations by Mary Ballachino
Photos provided courtesy of Michael Rutter

Library of Congress Cataloging-in-Publication Data
Rutter, Michael, 1953–
   Basic Essentials. Fly Fishing / Michael Rutter—1st ed.
      p. cm. — (Basic Essentials series)
   ISBN 0-7627-0955-3
      1. Fly fishing. I. Title: Fly Fishing. II. Title.

SH456.R8676 2001
799.1'24—dc21

2001033124

Manufactured in the United States of America
First Edition/First Printing

Contents

Acknowledgments   *iv*

1   Introduction to Fly Fishing   1

2   The *Essentials* of Equipment and Gear   5

3   The *Essentials* of the Cast   15

4   The *Essentials* of Reading Water   31

5   The *Essentials* of Presentation   39

6   The *Essentials* of Wet and Dry Flies   49

7   The *Essentials* of the Attractor Pattern   55

8   The *Essentials* of Trout   61

9   The *Essential* Largemouth, Smallmouth,
Panfish, and Walleye   67

10   The *Essentials* of Catch-and-Release   73

Index   75

Acknowledgments

I would like to acknowledge my fly-fishing brother, Casey Jones.
There's no one I'd rather throw dry flies with.

I'd like to thank Jon-Michael Rutter, fly-fishing pal and son, for his help
and support.

And Randi Swisher at Sage, I appreciate your help.

Introduction to Fly Fishing

What You'll Learn in This Book

Few things are more exciting than throwing a perfectly timed fly into a slow riffle on a gin-clear stream. Out of the current, a large cutthroat rises like a silver ghost, gulping your Royal Coachman.

You lift your rod, taking up the slack, setting the hook. The cutt turns and strips line off your reel as he runs. You manage to turn the silver bullet, taking back 10 feet of fly line before the fish runs again. You palm your reel, slowing him down. After three, five, or ten minutes—you're not sure—you land the heavy fish in the quiet water.

You appreciate the scarlet slash under his mouth, and the lovely collection of spots. You wink to the fish, wishing him well, cupping him gently as you return him to the water. With a swish of spotted tail, your trophy is gone.

It doesn't get any better.

In this book, I'm going to teach you how to catch fish with flies.

Fly fishing isn't hard, but it can be confusing. It's hard to know where to start. Throwing flies may seem a little mystical at first, but the passion we call fly casting looks more complex than it actually is.

In this book you'll learn the essentials:

- **You'll learn how to buy the right equipment,** including rod, reel, line, and other accessories, since fly fishing is a gear-oriented sport.

- **You'll learn how to cast your fly line** and how to set up your equipment so you're ready to fish—including important knots.

- **You'll learn how to "read the water"** to know where to start fishing. Consider this a crash course in learning how to think like a fish.

- **You'll learn about the bugs that fish eat**—and how to use flies to match your prey's natural food.

- **You'll learn how to present your fly naturally** so the fish will pick it up.

- **You'll learn about wet and dry flies**—how to tell them apart, and how each is fished.

- **You'll learn about the different types of fish**—about trout, along with bass and other warm-water species you can take with a fly.

- **You'll learn how to catch and release**—remember, a fish can be caught again and again.

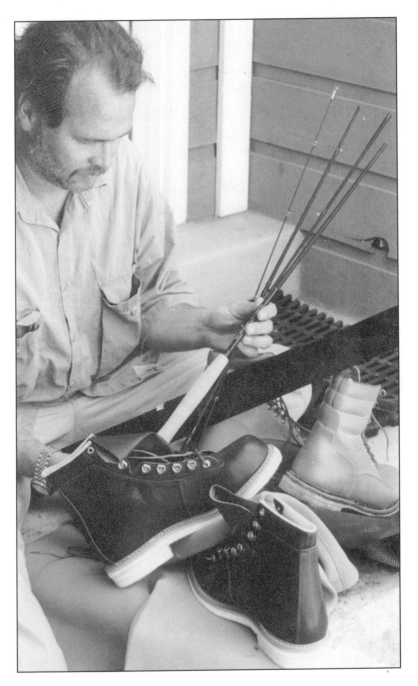

Figure 1

This book will help you sort through the maze of gear and show you what you need.

The *Essentials* of Equipment and Gear

Getting Set Up to Fish

L et's talk essential equipment and setup. You're itching to get on the water, and I don't blame you. However, before you step into the stream, you need to have the right stuff.

Fly fishing is gear oriented. It costs to get started. In this chapter I'll tell you what gear essentials you'll need to get on the water. I'll help you wade through the maze so you can make the best decision for the type of fly fishing you want to do (and for your budget). We'll talk about some other essentials, too. At the end of this chapter we'll look at how to get set up, specifically all the knots you'll need to know to help you tie up the loose ends (like fly lines and leaders).

The Fly Rod

A fly rod will be your single most important fly-casting investment. It will also be the most expensive. Rod selection should be a careful, thoughtful process. Choosing a rod is like getting married. Your rod will be an extension of your hand.

Most importantly, your rod casts and mends your fly line. But the rod also tells you when a fish is picking up your fly, when you've bumped the bottom, or when your fly is dragging. And it also acts as a shock absorber when you fight a fish.

Rods come in many styles and price ranges—from $20 to $2,000. You have to consider different lengths, weights, construction materials, and fishing orientations. If you've inherited an old rod or can borrow one, use it for a while until you've learned what you need. In the meanwhile, shop around for a good deal.

Fly Fishing

Figure 2

A good rod is your single most important investment.

Select a Rod for Water Conditions and for Fish

Select a rod to match your fishing conditions. . . a rod to match the fish you want to catch. A 5-, 6-, or 7-weight, 9-foot rod is a good all-around choice (the 5-weight rod is the lighter, the 7-weight heavier).

As a rule, lighter rods are for smaller fish; heavier rods are for bigger fish (or rougher conditions). It's not much fun to catch 12-inch trout on a heavy 9-weight salmon rod. Conversely, a 4-weight rod, ideal for small-stream trout, is hardly built to land a 10-pound largemouth.

If you're going to fish small, brushy streams where long casts aren't required, consider a shorter rod, such as a 4-weight 8-footer. A shorter rod is better when casting around brush. A lighter line weight will allow a more delicate presentation to the easily frightened fish here. If you're going to float-tube on lakes and ponds, look at a 5- or 6-weight 10-foot rod. You'll want a tall rod since you're sitting lower on the water—it'll help your cast. If you plan to catch larger fish, such as bass, you'll want a little heavier rod, perhaps a 7- or 8-weight. Delicate presentations usually aren't an issue; besides, a stronger rod will help you set the hook and turn the fish away from structure.

Decide what your needs are before you rush into a rod purchase. My favorite rod has always been a Sage 5-weight 9-footer—a good all-around choice for most casters. I've caught about every game fish in North America on this rod, but I enjoy catching big fish with light tackle (I also lose fish as a result).

Before you buy, visit several fishing or sporting goods stores and look at your options. See if they have rods that you can cast and compare. Pick up a number of rods and swish them through the air. Does the rod quickly recover (quit shaking)? Or does it feel like a shaking noodle? Does the rod feel good in your hand? Do you like the grip? Ask the salesperson to list the pros and cons of each model.

Other Rod Considerations

Sure, cost is a factor. I've lived on a budget too long to say it isn't. However, don't let cost be the only driver in your rod selection. You really do get what you pay for in a fly rod. Performance differences you may not notice right now will show up dramatically before long. I think it's better, and more cost effective, to buy a decent rod from the start. A cheap rod is a false economy.

There's a huge performance gap between cheap rods and good entry-level models made by serious fly-rod manufacturers. I'm not suggesting that you break the bank, but again, do start with a good piece of equipment. If you can't afford the rod you want now, wait until you can.

When you're shopping for a rod, stick with traditional names. Sage, G. Loomis, Orvis, Redington, and St. Croix all make serious entry-level rods priced from $115 to $225. Any of these rods will be a quality investment that performs for years.

I recommend a serious look at Sage's Discovery 2 for around $200. I think it's the best rod for the money, a rod that will serve you well, even into the expert stage. I use the Sage DS2 in corporate fly-casting seminars and have never had a complaint. It has excellent line speed. For a little bit more, consider the Sage VPS, an excellent intermediate rod that loads the line quickly (on the back cast) for efficient overall casting. Both of these rods are good investments since you can grow into them—and they'll last a lifetime.

Last but not least, don't walk out of the store without a rod case. Some come with a case; others don't. A rod without a case is a broken rod!

The Fly Line

After your rod, the fly line is your single most important piece of gear. It is literally your casting lifeline.

When you fish with a spinning rod, its action and the weight of the lure are what pull the line; the line is along for the ride. When you're fly casting, however, the weight of the line does the casting, and the fly is along for the ride. You need a good line.

Your first line will probably be a weight-forward (WF) floating (F) line matched to your rod. Let's learn why. Let's also cover some of the essentials you'll need to know about fly lines.

Matching Your Line to Your Rod

Every rod is designed to throw a certain line weight. It's important to stick with the rod's recommended line. For example, if your rod is a 5-weight, you need to throw a 5-weight line. If your rod is a 5/6, go with the higher line weight.

You can find this information written on the rod itself; it's just above the grip, usually next to the manufacturer's name.

Line Weight

Fly casters use the term *weight* when they talk about fly lines. It refers to how many grams are in the first 30 feet of the line.

A 4-weight line is, therefore, lighter than a 6-weight line. It stands to reason, then, that a rod built to throw a 3-weight line will not be effective if used to cast a 7-weight line. You can also understand that a 4-weight line, used for delicate casting, hits the water more softly than a heavy 9-weight line.

Line Tapers

Fly lines come in different shapes. The three that you need to be most concerned about are the level (L), the double taper (DT), and the weight forward (WF).

Unless your needs are specialized, a weight-forward (WF) line is your best bet. This line is the easiest to cast. Because of the way it's designed, with the lineweight concentrated in the forward section, it shoots smoothly and is rather forgiving. It's also the best line for casting in the wind.

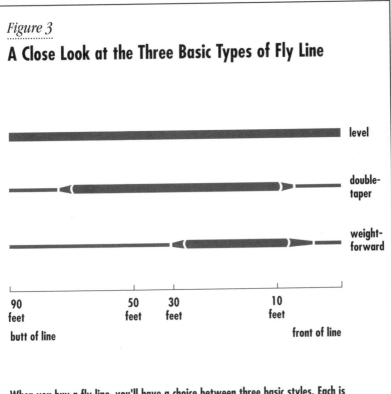

Figure 3

A Close Look at the Three Basic Types of Fly Line

level

double-taper

weight-forward

| 90 feet | | 50 feet | 30 feet | | 10 feet | |

butt of line   front of line

When you buy a fly line, you'll have a choice between three basic styles. Each is designed differently. A level line has no change in diameter. It's inexpensive—the line you'll often find with combination rod, reel, and line kits. It's difficult to cast, however, and I would avoid it. A double-taper has a casting taper at both ends, but no running line. It's thick and takes up a lot of reel space. It's also harder to cast distances with. The advantage is that its shallow taper makes it a good line for delicate casts. The weight-forward is my recommendation and the most popular line. (See next graphic.)

Figure 4

A Weight-Forward (WF) Line in More Detail

| running (shooting) line | back taper | belly | front taper | point |

A weight-forward (WF) line is excellent for beginners and experts. It loads well and is easier to control. Most of the weight is at the front—in the line's first 30 feet.

Line Action

Fly lines are built to either sink (S) or float (F). When you look at the package, it will tell you.

Your first line should be a *floating line*. As the name suggests, this line floats on the surface of the water. (It's made with tiny air bubbles to keep it buoyant.) This is the workhorse line of the fly caster. It's used for dry-fly fishing, but you can fish nymphs and streamers with it, too. (There's more on these different types of flies in later chapters.)

A *sinking line*, as you'd expect, sinks in the water. And depending on the line, it sinks at different speeds. If you need to get down to the fish, especially in ponds and lakes, a sinking line will be effective. A fast-sinking line is good for rivers with currents.

A *sinking tip line* has a tip that sinks quickly, but the rest of the line floats. This line is often used for steelhead and salmon in rivers. It's a specialized line and one you probably won't need to worry about for a while.

Backing

When you go to purchase your fly line, pick up a spool of backing, too. You don't connect your fly line directly to the reel; you connect it to its backing, which is in turn connected to the reel. There are two reasons for this. First, your fly line is only 75 to 100 feet long, so large fish could spool you (pull out all the line) on a good run. And second, your backing fills out the extra space on your reel.

To get your backing on correctly, reel the fly line on first. Then reel on the backing until it's ¼ *inch* from the lip of the reel. Cut the backing. Now pull off the backing and fly line. Tie the backing to the reel and connect the front of the backing to the butt of the fly line. You're all set.

Leader

The leader is a clear, tapered monofilament line that attaches to your fly line. You attach the heavier end of the leader to your fly line, tie your fly onto the thinner end of the leader. The tip, or tippet, of the leader comes in various strengths, known as *pound test*. You'll use different pound tests depending on the conditions and the fish you're after. Tippets are also classified by diameter, generally ranging from 8X (the thinnest) to 0X.

Buy several packs of leader material. As a rule, I prefer a soft leader with little memory. (Line memory refers to the tendency of hard nylon to come off a spool in coils, thereby preventing a natural presentation.) Scientific Anglers, Dai-Riki, and Orvis make good leaders.

The Fly Reel

If you need to cut corners, cut corners on your fly reel. You can always upgrade later.

A reel doesn't help you cast or mend, or make your presentation any better. A reel is a really nice place to hang your line. True, its drag is helpful when you're fighting a big fish, but you can always palm the line spool to slow it down.

For now almost any reel will do. I'd rather see you put your money into your line and rod. Nevertheless, let's examine fly reels in a little more detail.

Types of Fly Reels

Fly reels have different types of drag systems. The drag can be adjusted so it makes the line harder to pull. Thus, it can be set high or low. When you hook a big fish, the drag pressure wears him down as he strips out line.

Less expensive reels have a *pawl-click* drag system: There is a large gear with a pawl that fits into the notches. This pawl puts pressure on the gear and makes the line harder to pull. It's a simple reel. The less expensive it is, the more plastic it will have. These reels cost between $30 and $100. If you don't catch a lot of big fish (which demand a good drag), this pawl-click reel will do. Scientific Anglers makes several very nice models. The System 1 and Concept 1 are both workhorses that will last for decades.

A *disc-drag* reel is better made. The drag system is also more consistent since it works like a disc brake. A pawl-click drag applies pressure to only one section of a toothed gear, making the drag a little wobbly and uneven. The disc drag, however, applies even pressure, so it's smooth and a better choice for casters who seek larger fish. If you consistently seek big fish, a disc drag is critical. I recommend the Scientific Anglers System 2 disc-drag reel. Be forewarned: You probably won't wear it out in a lifetime.

Things to Look for in a Reel

- **Match your rod.** Look for a reel that's matched to your rod. If the reel is designed for 8-weight line, you wouldn't want to put it on a 4-weight rod. It would be too heavy and it would throw off the rod's balance.

- **Light weight.** Try to find the lightest reel you can within your budget. After a day on the water, the weight of a heavy reel starts to wear you out. A heavy reel can also throw off the balance of a nice rod. Be warned, though, that "light" is what starts to make a reel pricey. The Scientific Anglers System 2L is a very light reel for a good price. I've used two System 2L reels for the last ten years. I've put more than 1,200 fishing days on these two reels collectively, and except for scratches, they're still brand new.

- **Spool size.** Consider a large-arbor reel, which has a larger spool—very handy for large, running fish. The drag is more consistent; it recovers line quickly; and since the spool is larger, so the line isn't wrapped or coiled as tightly, you'll get less line memory. This will give you longer casts. Sage makes a wonderful large-arbor reel. I fish the Sage 3200, but I'm also fond of the Sage 3100 (made for very light rods).

- **Extra Spool.** When you buy a reel, consider an extra spool. As your fly-fishing experience grows, you'll want to try other types of line, and an extra spool allows you to do this. It's a perfect place to store that sinking line you've been wanting. You won't have to buy a second reel, and you'll be able to change lines quickly.

Waders

Unless you fly fish from a boat or in very small streams, you'll need to wade. Wading allows you to avoid the bush on the bank; also, and more importantly, being in the water gives you better casting position. Wading makes it easier to get an effective drift, too.

So you need some type of waders. (In mild weather you can wade in shorts, but you'll freeze if you try to fish this way year-round!) Waders come in two styles: *chest waders* and *hip waders*. Unless you fish only small, shallow streams, chest waders are pretty much the standard and the style I recommend.

Waders are also made from several different materials: *rubber, neoprene,* and *breathable fabrics*. Rubber waders are cheap and work for a season or two before they leak so badly you have to throw them away. They tend to drag in the water and are cold in cold weather. Neoprene waders cost a little more, fit more snugly so they don't drag, and are warm in colder weather. I've never gotten less than eight or ten years from a pair.

Breathable waders allow moisture to get out—but not in. That makes them warmer in winter and cooler in summer. They're made from Gore-Tex or a similar fabric and are very comfortable, though they do cost a little more than neoprene. In winter you can warm them up by wearing long johns and fleece underneath. If you can afford it, breathable is the best way to go, and for my money, Orvis is a fine value. This is the best wader on the market. Orvis, by the way, was a pioneer in breathable waders.

You have one more choice to make in waders: They come stocking footed (you have to purchase wading boots as well) or with the boots attached. A stocking-footed wader is, I think, the better route. You'll get a more comfortable fit. This will pay off when you walk to your fishing hole, stand for hours casting, or move about over slippery rocks. When you buy your boots, make sure you get the kind with felt pads (yes, they're replaceable). Felt soles give you a lot of traction on slippery rocks.

Accessories

You'll need some sort of vest or pack to carry your stuff. I've tried them all and gone back to the traditional vest with lots of pockets. Pick what works for you. I have two Orvis vests that are many years old and have worn like iron. They get more character as they get older.

Start by throwing in the following important items: a disposable rain poncho, sunscreen, lip balm, waterproof matches, a thin pair of gloves, and the Victorinox Swiss Army knife (I prefer the Champ with all the extras—I've used every one of them). Don't forget a hat and polarized glasses (these help you see into the water and cut glare).

You'll also need the following fishing necessities soon:

- Fly box(es) to hold your flies

- Flotant to dress your dry flies so they'll float

- Hemostat for removing flies from a fish's mouth

- Line nippers (fingernail clippers will work) for trimming line

- Sinkers (split shot in BB size and smaller) to weigh down wet flies

- Strike indicators for wet-fly fishing—they let you know when a fish has taken your fly

- Fishing net with a cotton basket (soft cotton is easy on fish)

- Counter Assault Bear Spray if you're fishing in bear country

- Tippet materials—various sizes of monofilament

Later, you might want to add a few more items: thermometer, hook sharpener, stomach pump (to see what's in a fish's stomach), and knot-tying devices.

The *Essentials* of the Cast

Getting Your Fly Where You Want It

Casting is an essential part of fly fishing. In this chapter I'll show you how to perform the basic cast so your fly goes where you want it to go.

Learning how to cast isn't as difficult as it looks if you follow the basic steps, but it does take a little practice. You can expect some bad casts at first. I should also point out that you don't have to be an expert caster to catch fish. Many beginning fly casters catch fish their first time on the water. Have fun. No caster is ever completely satisfied with his or her cast—it's something you'll work on for the rest of your life.

Things to Remember Before You Start

If casting gets frustrating, put down your rod, have a Coke, and come back in an hour or so. Also, review this list mentally every time you start to practice.

- Your fly line does what your rod tip tells it to do. That means *your rod tip must travel in a straight line.*

- Your rod tip does what your arm tells it to do. *If you drop your arm or your elbow slightly, your rod tip won't travel in a straight line and your cast will be off.*

- To keep your rod tip traveling correctly, tuck your elbow into your side so you don't drop the rod. *Later, when you master the basic cast, you won't need to do this.*

- As you practice, get in the habit of looking over your shoulder to see that the line is laying out behind you (I'll talk more about this later). Most casters start their forward cast too soon.

- Be aware of the size of the loops you're casting.

- Pick a target and aim for it.

- Don't try to throw too much line at once. *It's better to throw 20 or 30 feet of line effectively—most fish are caught at less than 30 feet.*

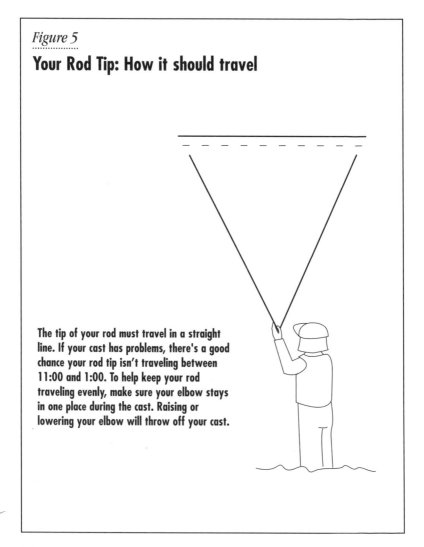

Figure 5

Your Rod Tip: How it should travel

The tip of your rod must travel in a straight line. If your cast has problems, there's a good chance your rod tip isn't traveling between 11:00 and 1:00. To help keep your rod traveling evenly, make sure your elbow stays in one place during the cast. Raising or lowering your elbow will throw off your cast.

Figure 6

Line Loops: Tight loop, Wide loop

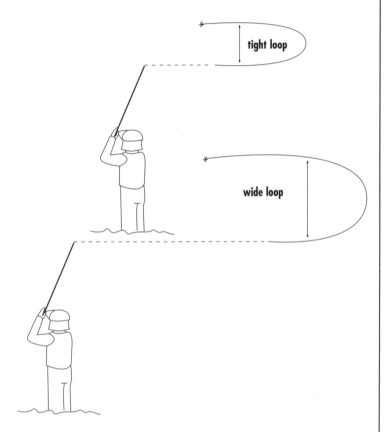

- A tight loop allows you a longer, more controlled cast. This is the favorite loop of the dry fly caster. To get a tighter loop, cast with an 11:30–to–12:30 motion. (Make sure you've mastered the traditional cast first.) You can also speed up you acceleration.
- A wide loop is often used for wet-fly fishing, when you're using a heavier fly. Increase the arc of your cast, cast from 10:30 to 1:30, and slow down the acceleration.

Figure 7

Rod grip is critical. Hold your thumb as shown. Tuck the line under your right index finger.

The Fly Caster's Grip

Before we talk about the specifics of casting, let's look at how to hold the fly rod—it makes all the difference. Look at the photo.

- Grip the rod loosely with the reel facing down.

- Your thumb should be pointing up the shaft of the rod.

- The line should be looped under your index finger. Get in the habit of *always* putting the fly line under your finger after you have cast—it helps you set the hook quickly.

The Casting Clock

Most beginning casters find it helpful to picture themselves casting next to a giant clock. Except when you shoot your line and fly at the target, *your rod tip will travel back between 11:00 and 1:00...then forward from 1:00 to 11:00.*

Before you strip out any line, grip your rod properly and practice moving between the two positions. You can practice on the water if you'd like; however, most casters find their backyards or a park a good place to start. Grass and water won't hurt your fly line; if you practice

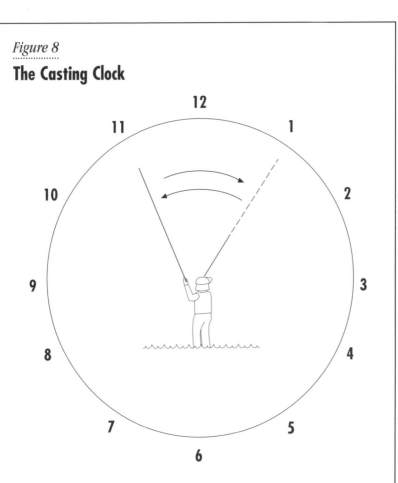

Figure 8

The Casting Clock

When you cast, pretend that you're standing in front of a large clock. The tip of your rod will travel back and forth between the 11:00 and 1:00 positions.

on the sidewalk or asphalt, however, it will wear out your line very rapidly. Clear at least 20 or 30 feet in front and in back of you.

You don't need to use a good leader for practice; a 9-foot section of any heavier mono will work. You can tie a fly to the end of the mono—be sure you clip off the hook unless you want a new earring. Or you can tie on a piece of yarn.

The Basic Backcast

The backcast is a little more difficult to master than the forward cast since you don't have eyes in the back of your head. The backcast is also the key to the forward cast, however, so it's where we'll begin. Until you learn how to feel your backcast (and it takes a while), get in the habit of looking over your shoulder and watching how your backcast lays out.

Carefully lay down your rod and strip off about 20 feet of line in front of you. (Don't be tempted to work with more line until you have this length mastered.) Now pick up the rod again and, remembering to keep an eye on your line loops, lift the line off the lawn and cast it behind you. Let the line drop for the time being. You'll put it all together later.

- Grip the rod correctly. There should be no slack in the fly line.

- Picture yourself next to the casting clock.

- Lift the line smoothly to 11:00. . . then pull the rod back, making sure that it travels in a straight line, until you get to 1:00. Stop the rod.

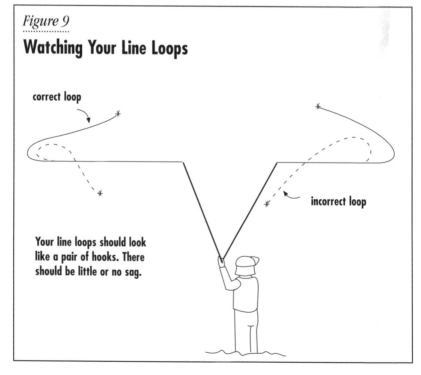

Figure 9

Watching Your Line Loops

correct loop

incorrect loop

Your line loops should look like a pair of hooks. There should be little or no sag.

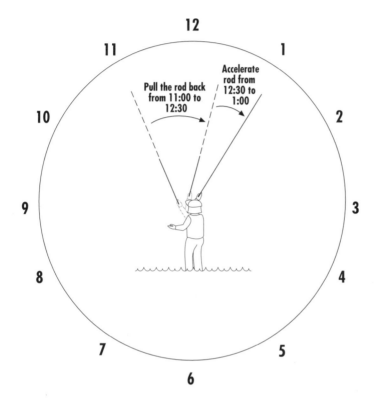

Figure 10
The Backcast

At the 11:00 position, pull the rod back without moving your elbow. When the tip of your rod gets to the 12:30 position—accelerate the motion of your rod (without moving your elbow). Stop the motion of your rod at 1:00. Pause at 1:00 while the line lays out behind you.

- Watch the line during your backcast. Still holding your rod at 1:00, let your line drift to the grass.

- Practice until the line starts to lay out flat (or sort of flat) behind you.

- After you begin to get the hang of the cast, work on accelerating harder between 12:00 and 1:00.

The Basic Forward Cast

Now let's work on the forward cast. Carefully lay down your rod and strip off 20 feet of line. Pick up the rod again, with the line behind you. On the stream, of course, you'd never start a cast like this, and having the line in back of you makes things even more awkward. Don't be too discouraged if your cast feels cumbersome.

- Make sure you're gripping the rod correctly. It should point behind you, with no slack in the fly line.

- Picture yourself next to the casting clock.

- In a fluid motion, lift the rod tip to 1:00. . . now accelerate your cast.

- Keep your rod tip traveling on an even plane.

- At 11:00 stop your cast and watch your fly line lay out in front of you.

- Let the line drift to the ground. Remember to hold your arm at 11:00.

- Practice until the line lays out flat in front of you (or sort of flat).

- After you start to get the hang of this cast, accelerate the thrust from 11:30 to 11:00.

Putting the Backcast and the Forward Cast Together

Before you put these two casts together, go back and practice them. In fact, anytime you have trouble putting the two casts into one fluid movement, you can go back and practice each step individually.

As I said earlier, the secret to the forward cast is a good backcast. *Make sure the line from your backcast has lain out completely before you start your forward cast.* If you hear a snap, your line hasn't lain out—you started your forward cast too soon. If your line puddles at your feet on the forward cast, your line hasn't lain out—you've started your forward cast too soon.

Now strip out about 20 feet of line in front of you:

- Grip the rod correctly. There should be no slack in the fly line.

- Picture yourself next to the casting clock.

- Lift the line smoothly to 11:00. . . then pull the rod back, and make sure it travels in a straight line, until you get to 1:00.

- Remember to accelerate the backward pull from 12:30 to 1:00—this keeps your loops tight.

Figure 11

The Forward Cast

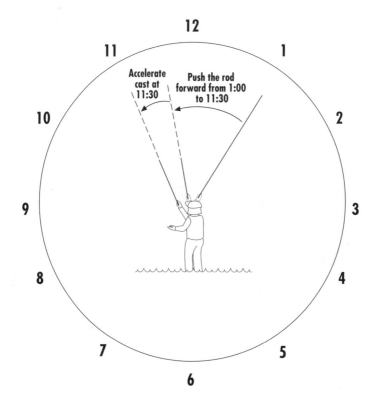

At the 1:00 position, push the rod forward without moving your elbow. When the tip of your rod gets to the 11:30 position, accelerate the motion of your rod (without moving your elbow). Stop the motion of your rod at 11:00. Pause at 11:00 while the line lays out in front of you.

- Watch the line during your backcast.

- When the line has lain out parallel to the ground—or is dropping slightly—execute the forward cast and stop at 11:00.

- Remember to accelerate the forward cast from 11:30 to 11:00.

- Hold the rod at 11:00 and watch the line lay out in front of you.

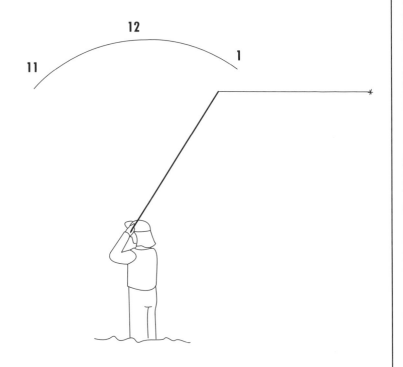

Figure 12

Casting Secrets: The Backcast

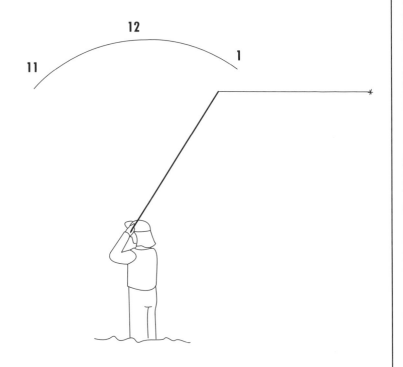

A good forward cast begins with a good backcast. Do not start the forward cast until the line is laying out flat (as shown). After executing the backcast, pause at 1:00. Many casters find it helpful to look over their shoulder to make sure the line is flat before starting the forward cast

- When the forward cast lays out parallel to the ground, execute the backcast.

Practice until your cast is fluid. You should be able to join dozens of forward and backcasts together after some practice. After you feel very comfortable working with 20 feet of fly line, add another 5 feet. Once you've mastered 25 feet, go to 30, and so on.

Delivery: Aiming Your Fly at a Target

When your forward and backcasts feel comfortable, it's time to work on delivery—that is, aiming your fly at a target. The first step is practicing what many casters call the *line drift*—letting the fly line and fly drift softly to the water (or in this case, lawn). At the same time that you do this, work on your aim.

Accuracy and soft line drift are more important than cast length. A person who can cast accurately with good line drift at 40 feet will always outfish the 90-foot caster who can't hit a target or get the fly down softly.

The key to this skill is practice and more practice. Your yard or the local park is a good place to start. When you do practice, place a target (an old gallon milk jug works nicely) about 25 to 30 feet away. Aim about three feet over the target. Don't move it back until you can hit it consistently.

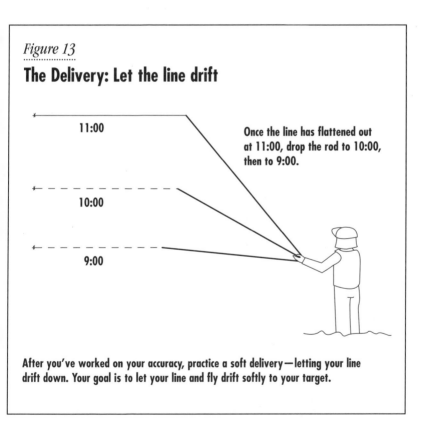

Figure 13

The Delivery: Let the line drift

11:00

Once the line has flattened out at 11:00, drop the rod to 10:00, then to 9:00.

10:00

9:00

After you've worked on your accuracy, practice a soft delivery—letting your line drift down. Your goal is to let your line and fly drift softly to your target.

Other Casts

There are many other casts you can learn, but they fall beyond the scope of a Basic Essentials book. Rest assured that you can fish for the rest of your life and catch a ton of fish on the basic cast you've just learned.

Still, one other cast might be particularly helpful: the *roll cast*. If you do a lot of wet-fly fishing, the roll cast will help you keep your fly

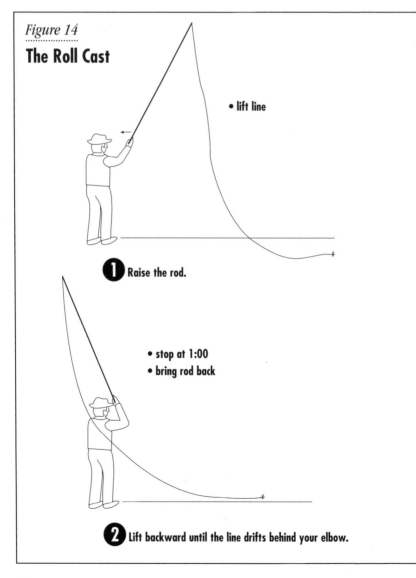

Figure 14

The Roll Cast

• lift line

1 Raise the rod.

• stop at 1:00
• bring rod back

2 Lift backward until the line drifts behind your elbow.

in the water longer. It's an easy cast to learn. Practice the steps on the lawn, but don't worry if it doesn't come together very well. It's one of those casts that require the friction of the water on the line to pull off. Next time the fishing is slow, try it out.

I'll talk about several mend casts later in the book when I discuss presentation.

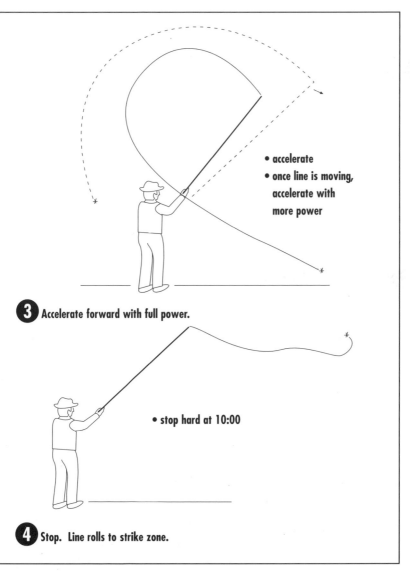

- accelerate
- once line is moving, accelerate with more power

3 Accelerate forward with full power.

- stop hard at 10:00

4 Stop. Line rolls to strike zone.

Knots You Need to Know

A discussion of casting seems to be the most logical place to talk about knots—you can't cast until stuff is tied up.

Knots are part of the fly-casting game and you'll be tying them often. I've included the basic knots you need to know to get started:

Figure 15

Improved Clinch Knot

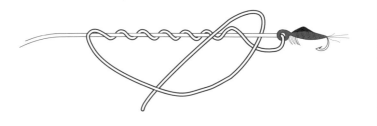

This is probably the knot used most often for tying the fly to the leader. (If you spit on the knot before you tighten, it will strengthen the knot.)

Figure 16

Surgeon's Knot

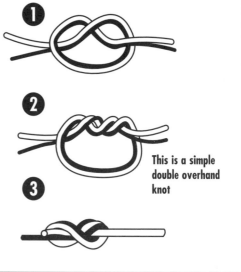

This is a good knot to know for tying your tippet to your leader. Moisten your knot before you tighten it to make it stronger.

This is a simple double overhand knot

Figure 17
Blood Knot

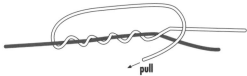

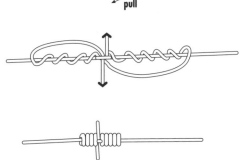

The blood knot joins together two mono lines. This knot maintains 91 percent of the line's breaking strength (that's very good). Because the knot is so streamlined, it runs through the guides very smoothly (making this a popular knot among casters).

Figure 18
Albright Knot

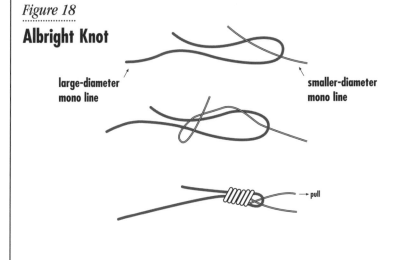

large-diameter mono line

smaller-diameter mono line

Occasionally you'll need to tie together two mono lines of highly unequal diameter. This easy knot is the best one I've found for the task.

Figure 19

Nail Knot

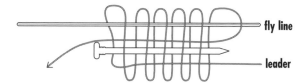

fly line

leader

fly line ⊂══════════════════⟋⟍⟍⟍⟍⟍► leader

**after tightening, your knot
should look like this**

**The best way to attach your leader to the fly line is with a nail knot. Tighten the line
around the nail. Then slip out the nail and tighten both sides of the leader.**

Most knots are pretty easy—you likely know some already. A few take a
little practice to master.

Knots can be used to tie your fly to the leader tippet (refer back to
the Improved Clinch Knot), the tippet to the leader (Surgeon's Knot,
Blood Knot, or Albright Knot), and the leader to the fly line (Nail Knot).
The Albright and the Nail Knot can also be used to tie the fly line to
the backing.

The *Essentials* of Reading Water

The ABCs of Finding Fish

I f there's one thing that separates catching from not catching, it's being able to read the water. This is probably the most important fishing skill you can learn. Being a great caster won't do you any good if you're not throwing flies where the fish are. Have you ever wondered why a handful of the fishermen (oops, fisherpersons) seem to catch all the fish? It's because they're fishing where the fish are. These folks know how to read the water! In this chapter I'm going to give you a crash course in life—from a fish's point of view.

Passive and Active Fish

Fish are on a never-ending quest for a full belly, but even these pea-brained critters can't be feeding all the time. Before you dive into the fish's home waters, you need to understand an important concept: Fish are either *passive* or *active*.

A passive fish, sometimes referred to as a *dormant* or *neutral* fish, is a fish that's not actively feeding. He might be resting, hiding, or trying to get or stay comfortable. There's a very good chance that a passive fish won't be holding where he feeds.

This fish isn't actively seeking food; however, he might nibble at something if it's right in front of him or looks like an easy meal. A passive fish can be caught, but you'll have to present your fly perfectly—and right before his nose. You'll have to work very hard to catch this fish.

An active fish is on the prowl for food and is easier to catch. He's hungry. He'll be where the food is. The active fish might be feeding

Fly Fishing Is a Thinking Person's Game

Don't rush into the water. Stop and look. Ask yourself these questions before you start casting:

• Where in the water will a fish be feeding?

• What is the fish feeding on?

• Where will a passive fish be resting?

• How can I wade in the water and cast a hook so I won't spook fish?

randomly, eating anything in sight that looks yummy (ants, nymphs, grasshoppers, caddis larvae). Or he might be feeding *selectively*, on one specific food and nothing else.

Fish Behavior in Rivers, Streams, Ponds, and Lakes

As I suggested earlier, it's foolish to simply plow into the water and start throwing line. You'll improve your cast, but you'll be lucky to hook a fish. To catch more fish, learn to *think* like our finned friends.

First of all, different types of water produce different feeding patterns. A fish in a river, stream, or creek will feed differently from a fish in stillwater—lakes and ponds.

As a rule, in moving water the current carries food to a fish. The fish selects a place where he can take food as it floats by. Ideally, this place is protected from the main current, safe from enemies, and close to the food source. A fish has to take in more calories than he burns staying in his feeding zone. This helps explain why an aggressive fish has to feed with a frenzy. Once he's full, he becomes passive and seeks a place to rest, burning as few calories as possible.

A lake or pond fish doesn't depend on the current. He has to search out his food, which burns up calories. An aggressive fish will patrol feeding zones. After feeding, he'll head back to safe water where he can hold, or rest, until he needs to feed again.

Again, a successful fly angler looks for feeding fish and casts to the aggressive ones. Sure, if you can't find feeding fish you can cast to a passive one, but the odds aren't as good. This is where reading the water

Figure 20

Look for fish near rocks and bridge pilings.

comes in: You look at the water and determine where you think the best fishing will be—and you fish there.

If fish are busting the surface for flies, or you can see them under the surface, half the battle is won. Often you don't have this luxury, though. You have to look at how the stream moves, how the water in the pond lies, the structure, the rocks. . . and determine where the fish might be.

Where Will a Fish Look for Food?

We all love to catch fish on the surface, lovingly referred to as dry-fly casting. There's magic in seeing a fish taking a topwater fly. However, most of the time fish do their eating *underneath* the surface.

Feeding fish hold on *seams*. A seam is a spot where the current is different, or the flow of the current is broken up or altered. Other obvious places are any sort of structure: rocks, fallen trees, cutbanks, the fronts or backs of sandbars, or small islands. In a stream, look for eddies and whirlpools where floating food is slowed down. Pay special attention to the backsides of rocks and boulders—the current is broken, so fish often hold here. In a stillwater, fish any sort of edge.

Figure 21

Where to Find Fish in a Stream

Look for fish close to undercuts

Look for fish at the heads of small feeder creeks

Look for fish on the lee side of boulders

Look for fish in riffles

Look for fish in the shade of trees and plants

Look for fish on the downstream side of snags

Look for fish where there is structure, a place for them to hide. Look for fish where the food is easiest to get. Seek out areas that provide fish with shelter, food, and protection.

Figure 22

Where to Find Fish in a Lake or Pond

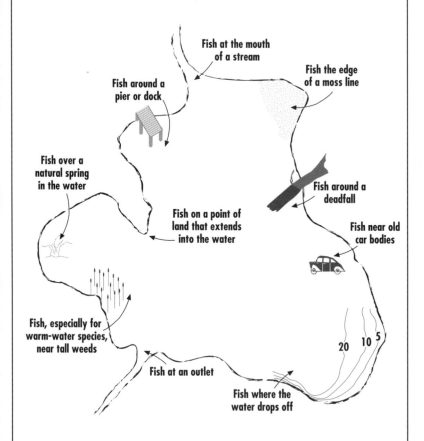

The key is fishing where the fish are. To do this, fish the edges: structure, boat docks, moss lines, drop-offs, inlets, or outlets. Watch for things fish might eat, and look for places a fish would feel safe.

Other Fish Considerations

Not all parts of a stream or stillwater are equal. Some are more likely than others to hold feeding fish. The time of year, insect hatches, volume of water, water temperature, and other factors all come into play.

- **Paranoia.** A fish is paranoid. Someone is always trying to eat him, which explains why he's so easily spooked. When a fish isn't eating, he's trying to keep from being eaten. The bigger a fish gets, the more jittery he becomes—which is why big fish are harder to catch than smaller ones.

- **Shadows.** A fish gets spooky in shallow or clear water—especially in direct sun. He knows that he's more vulnerable. This is why morning and evening tend to be good fishing times—the light is less direct, so fish feel more secure. This is also why a good angler spends a lot of time casting to the shady side of a bank, tree, or rock. Shadows offer greater safety and fish know it.

   When you see a fish in shallow or clear water, the feeding has to be pretty dang good to make it worth the risk. This is also why you have to be very careful with your own shadow when you're casting. A fish that's vulnerable won't give you a second chance. If he sees you, he's gone.

- **Deeper water.** The deeper the water, the more comfortable a fish feels—or at least safer from attack from above. This is why a passive fish will usually be found in a deeper part of the stream or lake. This is also why a spooked fish heads for cover in the deepest part of the water. The advantage to the caster is that the fish isn't as likely to spook here.

- **Temperature.** Our finned friends, like us, have ideal temperature ranges. If all things are equal, a fish will try to stay in water that meets his temperature requirements. This doesn't mean, though, that he won't go to warmer, less comfortable water to feed or find safety.

   A careful, successful fly caster knows the fish's ideal temperature zone and uses this to help locate them. This is also why a section of water that's good at one time of year might not be effective at another. The water is dynamic, and so are fish. If you can find a good food source near a fish's ideal temperature, you'll be successful.

Approximate Ideal Temperatures for Game Fish

Game Fish	Ideal Temperature Range (degrees Fahrenheit)
Brook trout	48-65
Brown trout	52-68
Rainbow trout	52-65
Cutthroat trout	50-64
Largemouth bass	70
Smallmouth bass	65
Walleye	65
Northern pike	64
Perch (Yellow)	63-65
Bluegill	72

- **Oxygen needs.** Humans breathe air. Fish breathe water—their gills extract oxygen from it. This is why temperature levels are so important for a fish: They breathe best at a certain water temperature. As the water grows warmer or cooler, a fish can't easily get the oxygen it needs. If the temperature is too extreme, the fish will die—literally suffocate in the water.

  You can get an idea how this feels when you're at high altitudes and gulping for breath—or in a hot steambath and getting barely enough air. In case you've forgotten, cool water holds oxygen better than warm water. And running water has more oxygen than calm water.

The *Essentials* of Presentation

The Fish Wants It Presented Nicely

The presentation of your fly is the final touch that will make or break your catching fish. You can have the best Sage rod money can buy, the finest, lightest reel, the most expensive line. You can have the best collection of hand-tied flies—flies that match the hatch perfectly. Your cast can be the stuff that dreams are made of, your loops tight and precise, your execution enviable and accurate. But if your presentation is off, your fly won't look natural to a waiting fish, and you won't catch a thing. This is why beginning fly anglers hear so much about "presenting their fly properly" from more experienced casters.

Good fly presentation is critical. I've discussed how to read the water in a previous chapter—learning where the fish will be holding. In this chapter I'll talk about how to present your fly to the fish so it will look natural. This includes fishing strategy and mending your line.

Breaking Down the Water

Many sports have a fair amount of terminology you have to master. I've avoided jargon as much as possible. However, when it comes to moving water, there are four major distinctions you need to be familiar with: *pools, runs, flats,* and *riffles.*

These are terms you'll encounter throughout your fly-fishing career. Knowing about each section (and its characteristics) will help you determine how you're going to fish a stream or river.

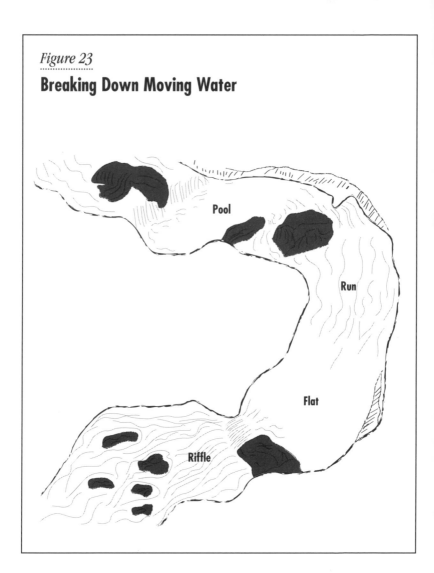

Figure 23
....

Breaking Down Moving Water

Pool

Run

Flat

Riffle

Pools

Pools are slow and deep sections of water. Often the fish in pools are large; however, such fish are frequently passive. A pool is thus a good place to try your bigger flies and streamers.

A pool can be subdivided into the *head,* the *middle,* and the *tail.* As a general rule, the head of the pool offers very good angling: Fish wait here for the food floating by on the current. There's often a bit of surface current and structure before the water flattens, so predators can't see a fish from above. The fish can hold without burning up a lot of calories.

The tail of the pool can be productive for aggressive fish, especially if there are safe places to hold—seams, rocks, drop-offs, structure. Often the water at the tail is shallow, so you can approach the fish without spooking them.

The middle of the pool, where the water is deepest, will hold resting or passive fish. The best way to fish a middle section is on the sides near a drop-off or wherever there's structure. Look for places where shallow and deep water come together. In places like this, active fish can get food easily but also retreat to safer water if need be.

Runs

A run (sometimes called a glide) is a smoother, calmer stretch of flowing water. Even though there are only a few ripples and swirls, the water is moving at a good pace. Rocks and structure provide shelter, and the water has a lot of oxygen. Don't think about what's going on on the surface, think about what's going on underneath. Use enough weight to get your fly down to the rough, rock-strewn, structure-strewn bottom.

Flats

A flat is a smooth stretch of flowing water. The bottom is also rather smooth. Because the water is easy to wade, you need to be careful not to spook the fish. Walk carefully; use a light tippet and a long leader with smaller flies.

Riffles

Riffles are fish feeding areas. The water isn't deep—no more than 4 feet. Fish in this water are aggressive and looking for food. Look for deeper pockets that hold fish.

Having a Fishing Strategy

Before you plow into the water and cast aimlessly, think about what you're doing and develop a fishing strategy. In other words, how are you going to fish a stretch of water?

First you need to read the water to determine where the fish are—or where you think they might be. Review Chapter 4, if you like. Look at the lake or stream, the structure, the way the water moves. Identify seams and currents. Get an idea where aggressive fish might wait or patrol for food, and where passive fish might rest. Once you've located fish (or potential fish), you can develop a plan for casting to them.

If you're not careful, especially if on a river or stream, you could easily foul a lot of good water before you begin to cast. Not only will you disturb the water you're fishing, but you could also spook fish up and down the stream. What do you think a few terrified fish zipping into the next stretch of water does? It spooks *those* fish, too. All it takes is one frightened fish effectively saying *The British are coming* to trigger a chain reaction in the water. Every aggressive fish for yards forgets about his tummy, becomes passive, and heads to the safest water until things calm down. You've shot yourself in the foot before you've even started to fish.

Effective fly casting is a thinking man's and woman's sport! There's nothing passive about it. It's proactive. You have to think all the time. You've read the water—but you can't stop there. Your goal is to have a marginal impact on the water you are fishing—or the water you plan to fish.

A Good Fly Caster Is a Thinker

Think before you enter the water. This isn't a board game, it's much more serious. It's you versus fish. Every action—or casting decision, in this case—has an opposite reaction, too. This is the ultimate game of strategy. Never mind that your quarry has a brain the size of a pea. He's also got the instincts of a wild animal, and he's in a never-ending fight for his life.

Think and plan before you enter the water. First of all, how are you going to get into the water without disturbing your finned foe? That means being aware of where your shadow is falling and the sound your footsteps are making on the bank. When you do enter the water, do so well above or below the target area you want to fish. Be quiet. Don't dislodge or bump rocks—sound waves travel very quickly in water.

Decide exactly where you'll start casting. Ask yourself some questions. What's the prime water? Where are the strike zones? What water will I cast to first? What other sections of the stream might hold fish—the edges, side waters? Do some stretches of water deserve more consideration? Should some be fished before others?

Bread-and-Butter Spots

There are certain parts of the water you need to pay special attention to. These are called the bread-and-butter spots—the water fish are most likely to haunt.

You'll want to cover these areas thoroughly. Some water only requires a cursory number of casts; if nothing happens, you move quickly to the next spot. In bread-and-butter spots, you'll keep fishing a little bit longer, even if you don't get a pickup. And you'll want to present your fly to every likely section of water—then target the suspected strike zone again in more detail. Adjust the weight on your fly so it gets to the bottom. You may also need to adjust the length of leader on your strike indicator. If fish aren't picking up the fly, change to a smaller or larger size. If you still aren't getting a strike, change patterns.

The Enemy Called Drag

Before I talk specifically about mending your fly line, I need to mention the enemy of fly casting: drag! Drag is the root of most presentation problems. Drag is, well, a drag.

What is drag? It's when your fly *moves, floats, or drifts unnaturally.* If your fly drags, it signals to the fish that it ain't real, and to leave it alone. Remember, a fish has spent his life watching stuff float on the current. He knows what floats naturally and what doesn't. If something comes downstream that looks good, but it drifts wrong, it's a complete turnoff. It can even spook a fish.

This is why you want your fly to drift naturally on the water. Even if your cast is perfect and your fly hits just above the possible strike zone, it's not enough. It's got to drift right. I hope I'm sounding like a broken record.

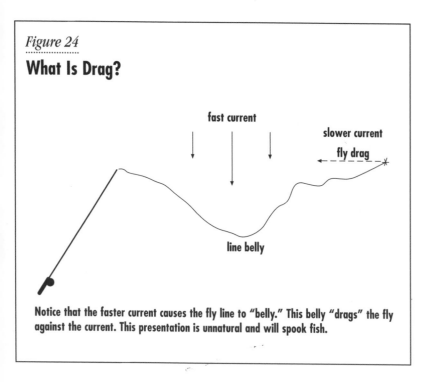

Figure 24

What Is Drag?

fast current

slower current

fly drag

line belly

Notice that the faster current causes the fly line to "belly." This belly "drags" the fly against the current. This presentation is unnatural and will spook fish.

Your fly will only drift the way your line tells it to. When you cast across a stretch of water, there are often different currents to contend with. If the current that hits the body of your line is faster than the current against your fly and leader, this will cause the line to "belly."

Bellying in turn will cause your fly to "drag" (skate, float, pull, drift, move, jerk, slide) unnaturally. Thus, your presentation is screwed up. Depending on the conditions, drag can range from slightly noticeable to dang awful. Unless a fish is extremely aggressive and has a death wish, even slightly noticeable drag will be enough to keep you from catching instead of casting.

Now, the good news: Unless the fish are spooky or the water shallow, if you muck up a drift, you can recast and try again. (If you mess up the drift several times, as we all do from time to time, you might want to try a different piece of water. The fish will be frightened.) Or you can try that other weapon in your fly-casting arsenal: the mend.

On-the-Water Mends

Remember that your fly line is rather heavy, while your fly and leader are very light. The fly and leader always follow the movement of the heavier fly line if the fly line is in stronger current. Here are the two most common mending scenarios you will encounter:

- *Your fly is in slower water and the body of your fly line is in faster water.* The faster water will belly the body of the heavier fly line, dragging the fly faster than it should be floating—if not pulling it sideways.

    To mend the drag: Flip the body of your fly line upcurrent so the faster current doesn't drag your fly (and leader).

- *Your fly is in faster water and the body of your fly line is in slower water.* The fly is going to drag or pull sideways. This looks unnatural to a waiting fish.

    To mend the drag: Flip the body of your fly line downcurrent so the slower current doesn't drag your fly (and leader).

These two variations are known collectively as the *reach mend.* Again, if the water on the body of the line is faster than that on the leader, throw the line upstream. If the water is slower, throw the line downstream. It's important to cast above the intended strike zone and start the mend before you get to the prime water—and continue to mend as often as you need to. Remember, too, that *you need to throw the mend before the fly starts to drag.* Depending on the current you're dealing with, you may need to throw a mend into your line every few

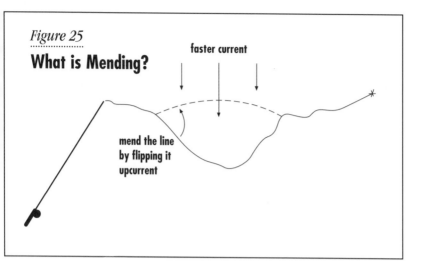

Figure 25

What is Mending?

faster current

mend the line
by flipping it
upcurrent

seconds to keep your drift natural. If the current isn't too strong, a single mend before your fly gets to the target zone might be enough.

It takes a little bit of practice to learn when you need to mend, but it will come quickly.

The secret of a smooth mend is taking up slack line, using the water's friction on the body of your fly line, and flipping with the rod tip. Having a good rod really pays off here. This is one reason I love my Sage rod. It's a fast-action model, and I can flip a mend effortlessly. This isn't possible with a less sensitive rod.

It's not always possible, but your goal is to try to throw the body of the fly line without disturbing the fly or leader. If you can't quite do this—and on some water it's very hard to pull off—make sure your mend occurs before your fly hits the strike zone.

Mend Casts

I've talked about mends you use while the line is on the water. Sometimes, though, you'll want to throw a mend into your line while you're executing your aiming cast. Your two mending-cast options here are the *reach mend cast* (left and right) and the *snake cast* (see illustrations on following pages).

These casts are especially useful if you are fishing tricky water with a narrow strike zone—and you might not have time to throw a mend. They're also good if you're afraid that an on-the-water mend might spook the fish.

Mend casts save time. They are also easy to do. With a little bit of practice, you can mend-cast like an expert.

Figure 26

Left Reach Cast Mend

Right Reach Cast Mend

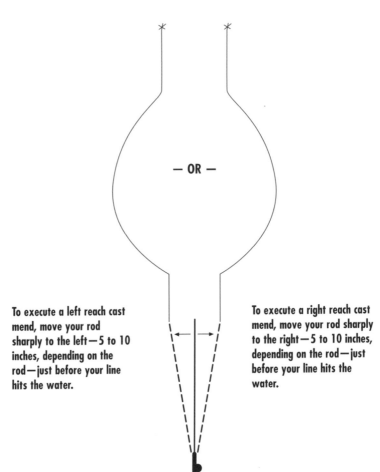

To execute a left reach cast mend, move your rod sharply to the left—5 to 10 inches, depending on the rod—just before your line hits the water.

To execute a right reach cast mend, move your rod sharply to the right—5 to 10 inches, depending on the rod—just before your line hits the water.

The reach cast mend is an excellent mend for faster water.

Figure 27

How to Execute the Snake Cast Mend

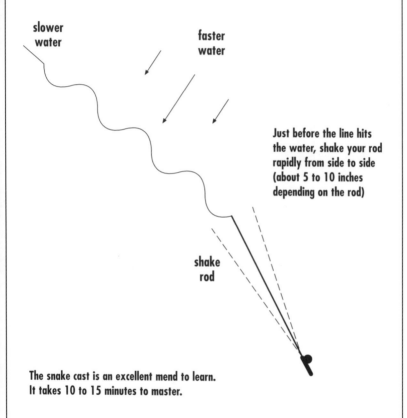

slower
water

faster
water

Just before the line hits
the water, shake your rod
rapidly from side to side
(about 5 to 10 inches
depending on the rod)

shake
rod

The snake cast is an excellent mend to learn.
It takes 10 to 15 minutes to master.

The *Essentials* of Wet and Dry Flies

Under the Water and On Top

As a fly caster you are practicing the art of illusion. You are trying to catch fish by *tricking* the fish into thinking your carefully crafted fly is real food.

Artificial flies are generally made out of yarn, thread, feathers, or fur. They might be tied together to resemble an insect trapped on the water such as a mayfly or caddis fly. Or they might be tied to look like a particular stage of an aquatic insect such as a caddis nymph or a floating crustacean. They might also be tied to resemble a minnow, frog, or even a mouse.

When you fly fish, especially if you are trying to fish a fly intended to imitate a specific insect, you need to consider the size, silhouette, and color of the natural fly in question. More importantly, you have to fish the fly exactly the way *the fish* expects it. If you don't fool it into thinking the fly is real food, you're not going to catch any fish.

I've talked briefly about wet and dry flies. Now let's take a more detailed look at these two categories. An old saying goes, "Dry-fly casters get all the glory, wet-fly casters get all the fish." Since fish feed under the water about 85 percent of the time, it pays to know how to fish a wet fly.

Most casters prefer to catch fish on the surface. There's a romance to dry fly casting that's hard to discount. However, since fish feed under water most of the time, you'll get pretty tired waiting for a hatch. Most casters do a little of both. When the hatch is on, enjoy it. When there's nothing on the surface, go deep.

The Differences Between Wet and Dry

When you fish a dry fly, you fish on the surface, or film, of the water.

Figure 28

Nymph

Figure 29

Streamer

Figure 30

Dry fly

When you fish a wet fly, you fish underneath the surface. The *manner* in which you fish the fly, not always the fly itself, determines the mode of fishing. If you're fishing on the film, you're dry-fly fishing. If you're fishing under the film, you're wet-fly fishing... even if you're using the same fly.

Still, there are differences between wet and dry flies. Some flies can cross over between wet and dry. Others are designed specifically for one purpose or another. Wet-fly hooks tend to be a little heavier and longer than dry-fly hooks. Generally speaking, wet flies are softer. Specifically, the hackles are softer. (They come from hens, not roosters.) A softer hackle gives the fly a more natural look in the water—making it come alive. A soft hackle undulates in the water, which looks enticing and lifelike to hungry fish. Also, wet flies usually have swept-back wings, making the fly more streamlined.

Dry flies have a stiff hackle (from roosters) to help them ride above the film. The wings are often high, too. Having a natural shape (not being streamlined or soft in the water) is most important.

Having a certain skill in casting is important to both wet and dry fishing. Nevertheless, casting skills are more critical for the dry-fly angler. If you're fishing wet flies, you can get away with a pretty sloppy cast—getting your line to the general area (even if it slaps, plops, and puddles). A dry-fly cast needs to be far more accurate and precise. You have to get your fly where you want it, and it must get there softly and delicately.

When you dry cast, you have to be careful. You're taking fish near the surface, and they will scare easily. Also, be sure the fish don't see you. When you take fish in deeper water, they feel safer and tend to be less spooky.

Tips on Fishing the Wet Fly

- **Leader and tippet.** The rod and reel you use for dry flies will work just fine for fishing wet. You'll likely want to use a shorter leader, though. You can trim down your dry leader. (Some casters like a stiffer leader for wets; try both and decide for yourself.) If you're using a sinking-tip line, streamers, or larger wet flies, use a shorter leader—4 to 5 feet. For heavier flies, use a 3X tippet. For nymphs, I like 6 or 7 feet—using a 4X tippet. Be sure to carry spools of tippet so you can add new line to your leader as needed. (Remember, the end of your leader gets smaller each time you tie on a new fly—after a few flies, you'll need to tie on more tippet.)

- **Weighting your fly.** Often, you'll want your wet fly on the bottom, where the fish are. Some wet flies are weighted—others aren't. Either way, you'll want to have split shot to weight your fly. Carry a variety of sizes, from micro shot to BB size. *Hint:* It's worthwhile to buy high-end shot, since it opens and closes much more easily.

  Most casters don't use enough weight. You need to feel your shot hitting the bottom. Yes, you're going to get hung up more, and yes, you'll collect moss and bottom gunk on every other cast, but you'll be down where the fish are. You'll be catching more fish.

- **Strike indicator.** A strike indicator is like a fly caster's bobber. It attaches to the top part of your leader—often just below the fly line. When you dry cast, you see the fish take the fly and you set the hook. When you wet fish, however, you watch your strike indicator. If it bobs, sinks, or moves counter to the current, set the hook. You can't see the leader, but you *can* see the indicator, which floats naturally on the current. When a fish picks up the fly, the indicator—well, indicates.

  A strike indicator also helps you with a good presentation. If it's

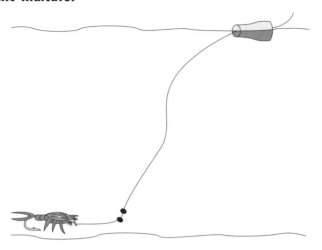

Figure 31

Strike Indicator

You'll increase your success when wet-fly casting by using a strike indicator. It shows (by sinking, by moving against the current, by moving unnaturally) that a fish might be on the fly. If the indicator moves, set the hook.

floating naturally, there's a good chance that your fly (which you can't see) is too. Thus, whenever you see any irregular bump in the strike indicator, set the hook. You'll do a lot of false setting, but some of the time you'll have a fish.

There are a lot of different kinds of strike indicators. The best is a piece of polypropylene yarn tied in a loop. It's very sensitive and drifts gracefully on the water. When I switched to this type of indicator, I caught 10 to 20 percent more fish—it's that sensitive. The next best is a disposable piece of sticky foam you wrap about your line.

- **Fishing the wet fly.** Read the water as carefully as you can. After you fish for a while, you'll get better at it. In the meantime, select a section of water and fish it thoroughly, casting to every likely spot as you work your way upstream. I think upstream is the best way to fish when you're starting. You'll get better drifts.

If you're quite sure there are fish in a section, take more time and cast carefully to it. After you start to understand this sport, you can stand in one place a little longer. For now, make slow, careful movements. And know when to quit: Too many beginning casters spend too much time in one stretch of water. If you happen to pick a fishless section, you don't want to cast to it all morning.

- **Nymph fishing.** When you nymph fish, dead-drift. Keep it as close to the bottom as you can. This makes for a more natural presentation.

- **Streamers.** A streamer is a wet fly designed to imitate a small fish. You give the life to a streamer. Work out a good pattern, experiment. If the fish are aggressive, a radical jerk will produce strikes. If the fish are selective or passive, slow it down. Small little twitches will be enough. Most casters work their streamers too hard. A little twitch is all you need.

Tips on Fishing the Dry Fly

Before I get more specific, let me say this: Your dry-fly cast has to be exact. If you fish a lot of drys, practice your cast and know your current limits. You have to get your line to the right place. But all things being equal, hitting a good hatch is like going to heaven.

- **Leader and tippet.** The rod and reel you use for wet casting will be just fine for drys. Presentation is everything. Your leader will need to be longer and more delicate. At the least, use a 9-foot leader (often longer).

- **Fishing the dry fly.** Surface-feeding fish are there to eat. This isn't comfortable water. They will frighten easily. Thus, use a light tippet. A fine tippet gives you a finer presentation. You're going to lose fish to breakoffs, but that's part of the game.

  You'll have to be very careful about where your fly line is—it can frighten fish, as can mending. And don't forget your shadow. Since your tippet is very fine, you'll need to change it often. Casting is critical. You'll need to cast far enough above the strike zone to get a perfect drift, but not so far above that you'll need to constantly mend.

  If at all possible, fish upstream and at an angle so that the body of your fly line is completely out of the fish's picture. If you're on a small stream or find the feeding fish above you, cast the fly line at least 2 to 4 feet downstream from the fish's tail. If it's any closer, it will likely scatter your fish. You'll need a long, delicate leader so that your fly (and leader) lands above the fish softly. If the leader is fine enough, it will pass over the fish, not scaring them, before the fly drifts by.

- **Rising fish.** The beauty of dry casting is you actually see the fish. The frustration is you can't always catch them—even though they're hopping all over the place. If you see feeding fish and can match the hatch, do so. Remember, if you think you've got the hatch matched but the fish come up, look at your fly, and don't take—go smaller!

  If you can't quite match the hatch, it doesn't always matter. Sometimes fish are in a feeding mode and will take everything in sight. Some great attractors you might try are the Adams, Royal Coachman, Royal Wulff, Mosquito, Gray Hackle Yellow, Elk Hair Caddis, and Black Gnat. (There's much more about attractors in the next chapter.)

  If the fish are really selective and you can't match the hatch, try attractors, or something entirely different. My recommendation would be a terrestrial—something large and calorie rich.

The *Essentials* of the Attractor Pattern

It Looks Good

An attractor pattern is a generic presentation that simply looks *buggy*. Apparently it looks like food to a fish, but it's a made-up pattern. Maybe it's a composite of several insects. It looks good, but it doesn't look like anything specific.

When you first start casting, you're trying to remember a number of things. You need to keep your loops tight, hook shaped, and small; your line has to hit the water softly. . . never mind that you're also trying to match the hatch. It's a lot to remember. As you juggle all these concepts at once, *attractor flies can be your best friends because they do catch fish.*

Let's explore attractor pattern.

Getting Started with Attractors

As you start to build up your fly box, attractor patterns are some of the first flies you ought to collect.

Some of the patterns I recommend come in different color variations. You might want to check with a fly shop or a seasoned caster in your area to see if one color seems to work better than another. Try that first. Eventually, you may want the pattern in several color phases. The following flies are not necessarily listed in order of their importance.

Dry-Fly Attractor Patterns You Should Carry

- **Adams** (#12-20). This is a must-have fly, good for trout and warm-water fish. It may be the best fly ever created—and it's become an all-time favorite attractor, too.

- **Humpy** (#10-16). Get this in yellow and red color phases. It's a good fly to throw when the fish are taking a specific insect, but you can't match it.

- **Royal Wulff** (#10-16). This excellent fly floats well and is a great standard; good for almost every type of fish.

- **Royal Coachman** (#14-20). A favorite. I caught my first fish on this fly; it's a great pattern for trout; and it floats well.

- **Renegade** (#10-18). Fish this wet or dry.

Nymph Attractor Patterns You Should Carry

- **Brassie** (#14-20). A great all-around pattern (both a specific and an attractor) that's an old favorite. Having a good selection to choose from is a must.

- **Serendipity** (#14-20). This is a very good attractor, especially as a chaser fly.

- **Hare's Ear** (#14-18). This specific has become an attractor. It looks good to fish; and it comes in a number of variations, sometimes with a beadhead—collect a good selection.

- **Pheasant Tail** (#14-18). Another specific that has become a fantastic attractor. It comes in a number of variations and in a beadhead—a good selection will pay off with lots of fish.

Streamer Attractor Patterns You Should Carry

- **Woolly Worm and Woolly Bugger** (#6-8). These aren't really streamers, but I'm putting them here because I often fish them like a streamer.

- **Muddler Minnow** (#6-10). This is a wonderful minnow attractor and a great pattern to have for almost any kind of fish.

- **Marabou Leech** (#2-16). This fly comes in a variety of colors; green, black, and brown are good choices. Marabou (a kind of feather) gives the pattern a lifelike quality in the water.

Fishing an Attractor Pattern

With drys, you'll generally dead-drift your attractor over the area where you think the fish are lying. If you're fishing through dead or stillwater and haven't been able to pull a rise from a fish, try an occasional twitch to attract attention. This simulates an insect fighting the current on the surface. But don't overdo it. A good twitch now and then will work wonders. One too many twitches and you can forget about catching a thing.

Wet flies are both dead-drifted and actively retrieved. Experiment with both techniques. As a rule of thumb, big fish often are attracted to more active prey. Woolly Buggers, Woolly Worms, and Muddlers are excellent patterns to animate with a twitch or a strip. (In fast water you'll probably want to dead-drift these patterns.)

Attractors for Bass and Warm-Water Fish

The patterns I've introduced so far were primarily designed for trout, but they'll work on all game fish, including bass. Trout generally take small bites and have smaller mouths than bass, so they usually require

Figure 32

Largemouth bass will take attractor flies.

smaller flies. More often than not, a trout takes a fly in a definitive fashion and fights like a freight train. Unlike a bass, which gobbles his prey, a trout will often take a hard look at the food before biting. When you dead-drift a nymph or present a dry fly on the film, it has to look natural.

A bass takes the fly like a freight train, and then fights like a freight train. He gulps. In fact, an 8-pound largemouth can take in almost a quart of water during a single gulp. When you fish for bass, you must fish the fly actively—bass like their food moving. The secret with largemouths is not the fly you choose but how you fish it.

Bass casting is the fastest growing segment of fly fishing. Many anglers are just discovering how much fun a bass can be on a fly rod. While I worship trout, I'm a bass boy, too. I've caught boatloads of largemouths on every fly suggested thus far. They work quite well.

However, there are other excellent bass flies tied specifically for wily largemouths. You'll want to collect them if you do much bass fishing. I'll get into more specifics later; for now, if you do bass fish, you'll find these useful:

- **Marabou Leech** (#6-14). Black, white, red, yellow, weighted or unweighted.

- **Muddler Minnow** (#1/0-10).

- **Grasshopper** (#4-12).

- **Deer Hair Popper** (#6-12).

- **Water Pup** (#6-8).

Depending on where you live, you might want to add crayfish, sculpin, and minnow patterns. (While they're often thought of as attractor patterns, crayfish can be fairly specific, too.)

All the suggestions made thus far will be deadly on panfish, too. Don't worry about crossing over. If you're going to do a lot of panfishing, you'll want to add a few flies to those I've mentioned. Patterns that have yellow in them seem especially good. You might consider:

- **Sponge Spider** (#8-12).

- **Deer Hair Popper** (#10-14).

- **Mickey Finn Bucktail** (#8-12). Weighted or unweighted.

- **Woolly Bugger** (#8-12). Black, white, weighted or unweighted.

- **Marabou Leech** (#10-14). Black, white, red, yellow, weighted or unweighted.

- **Leadwing Coachman** (#10-16). Weighted or unweighted.

- **Grasshopper** (#8-14).

In addition to these flies, consider other streamers, both bucktail and marabou, in a variety of colors and sizes. I like to fish for panfish with weighted flies, especially if I need to get deep. However, many casters prefer to use shot on the leader: They feel that it gives the fly a more natural feel. Try both and see what you think.

The *Essentials* of Trout

Why God Invented Fly Fishing

L et's take a look at the darling fish of the fly-casting community, the revered trout. The more you know about the fish you angle for, the more you'll catch. In the next few pages, I'm going to give you a crash course on trout.

Before I get trout specific, though, let me give you a few trout generalities. As a rule, trout are a little more delicate than most warm-water fish. Thus, they need to be handled carefully. Trout are also more oxygen sensitive and require cooler, cleaner water than many other types of fish.

You'll note that trout caught in clearer, cooler water are often distinctly marked; the colors are vivid and stunning. In contrast, fish living in dark, stained water often have a washed-out, dull color. During the spawn, trout are at their most exquisite—the colors vivid and vibrant.

The Brook Trout

Brook trout prefer water that's between 48 and 65 degrees Fahrenheit.

We call the brook trout a trout, but he's really a char (a cousin to the trout). With that said, let's look at this fish. The brookie has a greenish tint. His underside is a dull, creamy color, while the sides and fins have a dark reddish tint with dull ivory edges. There are wormlike markings on his back (a mark of the char, not the trout). Spots can be found along his sides, which have maroon centers.

In rivers and streams brookies can reach up to 4 pounds. In lakes they can grow up to 8 pounds. The average fish is 8 to 14 inches long. These East Coast natives have been transplanted, and do well in mountainous areas where the water is cold and clear. Brookies don't get as large as other species of trout. A 3- to 5-pound brookie is a big fish, while a 9- or a 10-pound brookie (found only in eastern Canada) is a monster.

When you hook this char, you won't get a fish that jumps out of the water like a rainbow. Instead, you get a good fighting fish that goes deep and will roll, trying to spit the hook. (More than once this has snapped the leader of a fly caster who counted his fish before it was netted.)

Brookies are not surface feeders like the rainbow or cutthroat. They'll come up if there's a hatch on, but they prefer to stay deeper in the water. They like to feed on other fish and can be very aggressive. A brook trout will take your fly with a vengeance and run like hell. For his size, he's a fighting fish.

This fish likes the security of deep water such as pools and back eddies. He'll move out into swift water, but only to feed; then he moves back quickly. Look in the shadows and near the deep water of undercut banks. In lakes look for underground springs and old river or stream channels.

This fish spawns during the latter part of summer in waters where winter comes quickly, and later in fall for waters farther south. Then the fish heads for gravelly riffle areas (or spring-fed waters in lakes).

The Brown Trout (German Brown)

Brown trout prefer water that's between 52 and 68 degrees Fahrenheit.

Browns are, well, brownish—ranging from a light chocolate to a silvery, dark chestnut. The underside of the fish is a lighter cream or yellow color. Black spots cover the body. Depending on the water and location, spot size and frequency will vary and be more or less noticeable. There are reddish spots with black borders on the fish's sides.

Fish in clear, cold water are usually more conclusively marked, and their colors are graphically apparent and striking. Browns living in dark, stained water will look washed out. During the spawn, the brown (as with all trout) is most winsome, with bright and vibrant colors. In rivers and streams brownies can reach 10 to 15 pounds. In lakes they can grow up to 30 pounds. The average fish is 12 to 18 inches long.

This fish is a transplant from Europe (the first came from Germany). They're thought of as nocturnal feeders (probably more so than other trout)—perhaps because some anglers presume that browns are difficult to catch. Such a reputation isn't entirely deserved. Certainly, browns are more light sensitive than any other trout. Mornings and evenings are the best times to fish for them.

The brown is an aggressive feeder. He eats anything that moves and is murder on minnows. The good news is that brown trout will readily

Figure 33

This female trout, or hen, is about to spawn. Get her back into the water as quickly as possible.

take flies. They're vicious topwater feeders, but don't overlook the wet fly. Browns feed heavily on aquatic life.

Browns love seclusion. Look for undercut banks, deep holes, and overhanging trees. Look for spots where there's shade on the water. Browns are probably the hardiest of all trout and can tolerate the warmest water. Often, you'll find browns in the lower reaches of a river, where the water is warmer and less oxygenated.

Browns spawn in fall. Look for gravel bottom in shallow water (1 to 3 feet) with a good flow of oxygenated water. During the spawn, the male develops a kyped, or hooked, jaw. At the same time, he gets very aggressive. This is the easiest time of year to hook a trophy-sized German brown.

The Cutthroat Trout

Cutthroats prefer water that's between 50 and 64 degrees Fahrenheit.

The cutthroat trout is a second cousin of the rainbow. There's a scarlet slash on the gill plate running under the throat and along the jaw. It's easy to see where he gets his name! In clear, cold water cutthroats are sharply marked: The scarlet is stunning and the spots are bold. In warmer, turbid water the fish look washed out and dull. The scarlet is bleached out and barely noticeable.

In rivers and streams a cutt can reach 6 to 10 pounds. In lakes he can grow up to 30 pounds. The average fish is 10 to 18 inches long.

When you hook into a cutthroat, you have a fish. Unlike his close cousin the rainbow trout, this fish probably won't jump. If you're lucky, a fighting cutthroat will roll on the surface, but nearly always he will dive. For this fish, depth is safety.

The cutt is the native son of the intermountain West. The Rocky Mountains and the Great Basin were originally all cutthroat waters until other fish were introduced (just as the rainbow was the fish of the West Coast). When stocking and transplanting occurred, all original ranges shifted, and those species that adapted the best remained. In many waters the cutt has a hard time competing with the 'bow and, especially, the German brown.

Cutthroat trout feed mostly on aquatic bugs and terrestrials. Those that live in lakes, where they can grow large, are often fierce predators, munching on any small fish in sight. Terrestrial patterns are deadly. There's nothing a cutt loves more than a good hopper or beetle. During spawns, egg patterns will be very useful.

Cutts haunt many of the same waters as rainbows—although they're less likely to be holding in front of a rock or in heavy riffles. Look for this fish at the bottom of the riffle and behind rocks that break up the flow of the current.

This fish will spawn in spring or early summer, depending on the water temperature and how far north it is. During the spawn, the cutts, especially if they're lake or pond fish, will move up tributaries and spawn in 1 to 2 feet of water over pea-sized gravel. Often this fish will cross with its cousin the rainbow. The result is a cutbow.

The Rainbow Trout

Rainbows prefer water that's between 52 and 65 degrees Fahrenheit.

This fish is a silvery color with a hint of green on his back. Colors vary: Some are dark, while others are almost dime bright. Rainbows have black spots scattered about their bodies and, depending on the water, the spots are more or less noticeable. Along the trout's sides is a rainbowlike streak of pinks and reds (which gives the fish his name).

In rivers and streams the rainbow can reach 10 to 15 pounds. In lakes he can grow up to 30 pounds. The average fish will be 10 to 16 inches long.

These fish are native of the Pacific Northwest but are now distributed widely—they can be found almost anywhere, since they're so

Figure 34
....

This wonderful rainbow was taken on a large Adams pattern at Flamingo Gorge Reservoir, Wyoming. We float-tubed the many inlets, casting to the shallow water where the fish were feeding.

hardy. As a result, they may be the most important trout for fisheries and anglers in general. They seem to thrive in hatcheries and take transporting quite well.

Rainbows feed on aquatic insects, terrestrials, and minnows. They feed very well topwater and are loved by dry-fly casters. The 'bow is also a lover of eggs: He's notorious for eating the eggs of all spawning fish. Egg patterns will take this stalking fish year-round. As the 'bow gets larger, he becomes more and more predatory toward other fish.

'Bows often lie in the middle of the stream and in riffles. They're as likely to lie in front of a rock as behind it. During spawning season, rainbows love to hold below spawning beds, where they pick up on the eggs drifting in the current.

Remember that rainbow trout like oxygenated water—which is why they'll be found in swifter water.

Depending on how far north you are, the wild rainbow spawns in spring. When a lot of hatchery fish have been introduced into a water system, the planters might spawn any time of year. Look for gravel bars (from pea to silver dollar sized) in 1 to 2 feet of water. In these areas spawning fish are sometimes stacked together as thick as cordwood.

The *Essential* Largemouth, Smallmouth, Panfish, and Walleye

The Other Fish That Take a Fly

T raditionally, trout have been the prey of the fly caster. Things have changed—for the better. Casters have discovered a new world of fishing pleasure. Let's take a look at how to take these "other" fish on a fly rod. You're in for some exciting times.

The Largemouth Bass

A bass is an *ambusher*. He lies behind a likely piece of structure and waits for his food. Then, with a short burst of speed, he gulps. Because bass live in so many different kinds of water, their coloration varies. In clear water the colors are brighter and more vivid, sometimes bright as a dime. In darker, murky water the color is a dull green ivory. In some waters the fish has a fairly green appearance, and the dark lines on the sides are more pronounced.

When bass casting, you're trying to entice, or trigger, a response. A fish will take your pattern either because it looks good or because it provokes his aggressive instincts. Like many aggressive, predatory fish, bass are a little nearsighted. This is one reason why twitching and moving the fly is so important—it allows the bass to home in on his prey.

Bass are assertive creatures—even downright offensive. Even if a largemouth isn't hungry, he doesn't like his private space invaded and will attack. During the spawn, it's worse. When the male is tending the nest, anything in sight gets attacked. Take advantage of this. Drift a pattern by, and you'll get a strike.

With trout, once you've hooked a fish, the water often goes dead for a while. The thrashing and movement frequently spook wary trout. Such activity, however, excites bass. If you catch one fish, keep fishing the same water. You might pick up another one.

How you work the fly will trigger either a hunger or an aggression response. Bass are big-bellied bullies to the core. They love to pick on whatever looks weak and struggling.

Competition is also another trigger for this finned bully. If one bass wants something—your twitching fly, for example—another bass will see the commotion and want it more. They'll fight to see which one gets there first.

When you read the water and look for structure, also keep in mind the water temperature. If the water becomes too hot or too cold, fish will get sluggish. When the water is cold, look for bass in shallower spots. When the water is warm or hot, they'll hold deep except to come up and feed. As a rule, in spring and fall fish are in shallow water. In summer they're deeper—unless you can catch them when they come in to eat. Adjust your fishing to where the fish are.

Bass have a pretty wide temperature zone, from about 35 to 90 degrees Fahrenheit. They're most active in water that's in the 70s; they'll feed actively in water in the low 80s.

Bass = structure! Find structure to find bass. Remember, they like to hide so they can ambush and hunt. Look near snags, by rocks, in the shadows, in weeds, on the shady side of weeds, near moss, under docks, or on a ledge. Look for places a fish can hide yet still see well enough to ambush a meal. If you've ever watched bass in clear water, you'll know they seem to come out of nowhere and take a pattern hard.

Bass-Fishing Gear

Any equipment you have will work for bass, but some gear will work better than others. You'll need a stiffer rod to set the hook—that mouth is hard. Also, a bass is a big-bodied fish and can be hard to turn in the water. Since you're fishing in waters that have a lot of structure, and thus a lot of potential hookups, you need a rod that allows you to horse your fly if it's hung up. A sensitive 5- or 6-weight rod can be used, but it's not ideal. A 7- or 8-weight might be a better choice.

A floating weight-forward line is my choice. Make sure you have a lot of backing on your reel. Your leader must be a little stiffer (you're throwing big flies)—perhaps a 1X. The average length would be 7½ to 9 feet. You might go shorter if you're using a wet fly.

Most of the flies you use will be from #2 through #10. For wet bass flies, your first choice should be large flies that imitate baitfish, frogs, leeches, polliwogs, hoppers, crickets, and crayfish. Here's a start for your fly box:

- **Deer Hair Popper** (#1/0-8).

- **Marabou Leech** (#1-8). Green, white, black.

- **Crayfish** (#1/0-6).

- **Joe's Hopper** (#2-10).

- **Zug Bug** (#8-14).

- **Marabou Muddler Minnow** (#6-8).

- **Bucktail streamers** (#2-10). Any color.

- **Sculpin Minnow** (#1/0-6).

- **Frog** (#2-6).

The Smallmouth Bass

How do you tell a smallmouth from a largemouth? Look at the fish's eye. Draw an imaginary line straight down. If the jaw extends beyond the eye, it's a largemouth. If not, it's a smallie (also, there is no horizontal black bar along the side). In small fish the eyes are very large. Smallmouths have dim spots on their sides.

As smallies grow older, they take on a more green-gold-bronze color. Of course, the intensity of the color varies with the water clarity and temperature. In more stained water a smallmouth will be less green tinted and a little more bronze yellow.

Smallmouth bass like cooler water. Their ideal temperature range is from 64 to 76 degrees Fahrenheit. Remember, they don't like competition, so if necessary they can push their optimum temperature zone without dramatic effects. They can function well in warm water if they have to.

Like most fish, the smallmouth bass is an opportunist—if it looks good, no matter when or where, there's a chance that he'll take it. This is very good news for the fly caster. Anytime can be feeding time. Depending on the body of water and the opportunity, a smallmouth bass will eat crayfish, hellgrammites, sculpins, waterdogs, frogs, rough fry (shiners, smelt, perch, char), game fry, mayflies, caddis, stoneflies, damsel flies, and dragonflies.

Figure 35

A nice smallie.

How to Fish for Smallmouths

Look for structure. Smallmouths move toward physical objects or hide in shadows. In rivers, streams, and lakes, look for cracks in rocks, outcropping branches, and logs. Look for a rock face that has plenty of corners and angles that extend into the water. A slide is always good. Look for a moss bank or a sunken log.

Don't worry about the strike zone or the perfect drift. These fish aren't picky. Try casting just above a fish's nose—it will trigger a response. Also try dead-drifting nymphs in front of the fish. The take is very subtle; you have to watch closely in order to set the hook.

Start your fishing around areas that break the flow of the current. The key to success with smallmouth is understanding what's going on at the bottom as well as at the top.

It's important to manipulate the fly. If you've fished streamers before, you'll have an advantage. Work the fly in a progressive pattern. Let the pattern stop, then pick it up again. Remember, a predator is a predator. Some of my favorite stream flies are hellgrammite, stonefly, hopper, and large Nymph patterns.

A 5- to 7-weight rod is standard. If you fish in water with a lot of structure or for bigger fish, a heavier rod would be useful. A floating weight-forward line is my choice. A sinking line will be necessary if you're fishing in deep water. Leaders should be 4X to 2X in 9-foot lengths. Your leader/tippet requirements will vary depending on the conditions. In clear waters you might need to tie on a fine, long leader. When you fish wet, you'll want to shorten up the leader.

Almost any fly that works for a largemouth will work for a smallmouth bass if it's downsized a little. Consider these flies:

- **Deer Hair Popper** (#2-8). Great for top water.

- **Hellgrammite Nymph** (#4-10). Great for bottom fishing.

- **Marabou Leech** (#2-12). Green, black, brown; an effective streamer.

- **Joe's Hopper** (#2-14). My favorite hopper pattern.

- **Crayfish** (#1-4). This is a favorite fly, a must-have.

- **Muddler Minnow** (#1/0-8). Looks like a minnow.

- **Zug Bug** (#8-14).

- **Marabou Minnow** (#6-8). Lifelike in the water.

- **Bucktail streamer** (#2-14). All colors.

Panfish

These fish are fighters, but they're also predators. You'll want to look for hiding places: weed beds, shelves, snags, docks, old cars, tires. It's a joy to take a panfish off the surface. Most of the time, however, you'll need to fish wet flies.

Because these fish are smaller, their mouths are also smaller. You'll need to use a smaller hook and pattern. This is also a good time to break out a smaller rod if you have one (3-weight and up). The lighter the rod, the more action you'll feel. Your presentation need not be delicate, either. A good solid plop on the water is a good calling card. Consider some of these traditional flies:

- **Deer Hair Popper** (#6-12).

- **Marabou Leech** (#4-14). Black, green, red, white.

- **Bucktail Wing** (#6-14).

- **Goddard Classic** (#12–14).

- **Woolly Worm** (#8–14). Green, black.

- **Gold Ribbed Hare's Ear** (#12–18).

Walleye

These elusive fish aren't great fly-rod quarry—but they can be caught. Walleyes are predators, and they eat other fish. Any minnow patterns are effective.

For smaller fish (the 1- to 2-pound range), you can be successful if you dead-drift nymph patterns with the current. The pickup is soft, so be ready to set the hook. Your fly will have to drift very naturally. Walleyes can be fussy about drag and drift.

You can also fish for them aggressively with a streamer or a minnow pattern. You'll need to experiment with depth. Then find out where the fish are holding. Experiment dragging and stripping your fly past the fish's nose. Experiment with the retrieve, too—start softly and work progressively from there.

You'll need a 5- to 8-weight rod with a reel that has good backing. I caught a 10-pounder during the spawn that stripped my backing down to the knot. I chased him downstream for 200 yards. I like a 7-weight rod that will set a hook into that bony mouth.

The best time to take walleyes is during the spawn when they come into the shallows. Favorite waters are feeder streams. At times larger fish seem to prefer a livelier retrieve; at other times they want a slow twitch. There are no set rules with walleyes. Experiment with your retrieve. My favorite walleye patterns:

- **Woolly Bugger** (#4–1/0). All colors.

- **Zonker** (#4–1/0).

- **Matuka** (#4–1/0).

- **Marabou Leech** (#8–1/0).

The *Essentials* of Catch-and-Release

Getting 'Em Back Unharmed

A fish is too valuable to catch only once. In fact, as the population of fishermen and -women grows, it stands to reason that there will be more and more catch-and-release waters.

I'm not saying you should never kill a fish for the pan or keep a trophy for your wall. But think first. Look at the water. Will it hurt the system if you take a fish? Is there a lot of fishing pressure in the area? How long does it take a fish to grow? Are the fish planters or wild?

If you have a choice, keep the planters—let the natives go. Planters are often dull and stupid—they deserve to be eaten. Catching a native fish is more challenging and satisfying. This is a fish suited for the water.

With possible exception of salmon and steelhead, there are few times when you're justified in taking and killing a fish during the spawn. It would be a shame to kill a fish before it had a chance to lay or fertilize eggs.

Unless you're dealing with a bumper crop (or panfish), take only enough for a meal. Don't fill your freezer. Fishing might have been cost effective in the old days when you dug some worms and headed for the local pond, but it's not anymore.

Effective Catch-and-Release

- Play the fish as quickly as you can. If the fish is worn out, he's more stressed and has a reduced chance of surviving. Remember, fighting is burning up energy.

Figure 36

Using a hemostat makes hook removal easier and faster.

- Netting a fish allows you to land him faster. However, make sure you use a cotton-basket net. A nylon-basket net might be abrasive.

- Wet your hands before grabbing the fish. Otherwise you'll take off his protective slime.

- If you can release the fly while the fish is still in the water, do so. The less you handle the fish, the better.

- If you don't have a net, grab the fish firmly, but not too hard. Turn trout over on their backs. This settles them down a bit. Grab a bass by the lower lip.

- Use barbless hooks or crimp down the barbs.

- Don't horse the hook out. Use hemostats. It's easier and faster.

- If the hook is in too deep, cut the line. The juices in the fish's mouth will eventually dissolve the metal hook.

- Never release the fish into a swift current.

- Gently release the fish, headfirst, into the current. Hold your hand under the fish. When he swims away, let him go.

- If he doesn't swim off, hold your hand under the fish near the tail and continue rocking him back and forth (moving water through his gills) until he gets his breath (fish CPR).

Index

A

Accessories, 13–14
Attracting-Pattern Flies, 55–59
  how to fish, 57
  for panfish, 71–72
  for trout, 57–59

B

Backcast 20–21
  combined with front cast, 22–24
  description of basic, 20
Backing, 10
Bass, attracting-pattern flies for, 57–59
Bass largemouth, 67–69
  aggressiveness of, 62
  characteristics, 62
  tackle for, 68–69
Bass, smallmouth, 69–71
  aggressiveness of, 69–71
  characteristic, 69–71
  tackle for, 71
Brook trout, 61–62
Brown trout, 62–63

C

Casting, 15–27
  backcast, 20–21
  combining front and
  back cast, 22–24
  delivery, 25
  forward cast, 22

  grip, 18
  mending, 44–47
  roll, 26–27
Casting clock, 18–19
Catch-and-release, 73–74
Chest waders, 12–13
Cutthroat trout, 63–64

D

Double taper, 9
Dry-fly, 51, 54–55
Dry-fly casting, 53–54
  drag, 43–44

E

Equipment, 5–14
  accessories, 13–14
  fly-line, 8–11
  reels, 11–12
  rods, 5–8
  waders, 12–13

F

Fish behavior, 31–35, 41–42
Flies, types to use, 49–51
Flotant, 13
Floating line, 10
Fly line(s), 8–11
  action, 10
Forward cast, 22–24

G

German brown trout, 62–63
Grip, 18

K

Knots, 28–30

L

Lakes, fishing in, 32–33, 35
Leader/spools of leader, 11

M

Mending, 44–47

N

Netting, 74
Nymph fishing, 53

O

Oxygen, 37

P

Panfish, 71–72
Pools, fishing in, 39–41

R

Rainbow trout, 64–65
Reach cast, 45–47
Reels, 11–12
  pawl-click, 11
  selection of, 12
Riffles, 39–41

Rods, 5–8
  length of, 7
  role of, 5
  selection of, based on fish and
water conditions, 7
Runs, 39–41

S

Shadows, 36
Sinking line, 10
Smallmouth bass, 69–71
Snake cast mend, 45, 47
Streamers, 53
Strike indicator, 51–52

T

Temperature, 36–37
Tippet, 14, 51
Trout, 61–65
  brook, 61–62
  cutthroat, 63–64
  German brown, 62–63
  rainbow, 64–65

W

Walleye, 72
Waders, 12–13
  built-in boots, 13
  chest, 13
  hip, 13
  neoprene, 13
  rubber, 13
Weight forward line, 9–10
Weighing fly, 51
Wet fly, 51–53